The Size of the Horizon, or, I Explained Everything to the Trees

The Size of the Horizon, or, I Explained Everything to the Trees

poems

Mitchell Nobis

Chicago | Los Angeles

The Size of the Horizon, or, I Explained Everything to the Trees

Published in the United States by Match Factory Editions, 2025

ISBN 978-1-966253-10-5 (hardcover)
ISBN 978-1-966253-09-9 (paperback)
ISBN 978-1-966253-11-2 (ebook)

Library of Congress Control Number: 2025932465

matchfactoryeditions.com

Book layout by RD Morgan

Cover art and design by Gretchen Hasse

Colophon design by Randy Cochran

For my parents.
Words are not enough, but thank you for everything.

"At a restaurant I overheard a guy say to the waiter 'Can you put a rush on my fajitas, I'm DJing at 10' and it suddenly occurred to me just 500 million years ago we were all just microscopic particles crashing into each other in a vast ocean."

—Matt Oswalt

Table of Contents

1

2

3

4

5

6

1

The Trees

I.

America,
I've been trying to write a poem
about trees for three days,
but America,
you keep shooting people.
I want my boys
to appreciate the trees too,
but how am I supposed
to teach them about the trees
when I don't even know
how to keep my boys alive?
I do my part.
I feed them. Hug them.
Teach them how to treat
others with love.
I play basketball with them. Snuggle them.
Teach them the difference
between right and wrong.
And America,
you make that last one hard.
I want my boys
to know the woods, to know some rivers,
to have some favorite books,
but America,
it's awfully distracting
that you keep shooting people.
I've been trying to write a poem
about trees for three days,

but I can't,
America,
when you shoot up another school &
show a Black man getting shot
live online by an officer
but let his killer go free—
both of those in just this week.

Someone said "what is it when
a death is ruled a homicide but
no one is responsible for it"
and America,
that's a helluva good question.
How do I teach my boys about trees
when we don't have an answer
for that.

I want my boys
to know right from wrong,
and most of us have a good
grasp on what that is,
but America,
why don't you?
I want my boys
to know that they matter.
I want my boys
to enjoy this life too.
And that's easy right now when
everyone thinks they're cute,
but what happens
when they're taller than you,
America,
and need deodorant
and their skin becomes a weapon
and their hair becomes a threat

to you.
I want my boys
to solve problems with
thinking and words.
I want my boys
to love you.
America,
I've been trying to write a poem
about trees for three days,
but you keep shooting people.
America,
you keep letting people shoot people.
I want my boys,
America.
Leave me my boys
I want my boys
I want my boys

II.

It's not us. Turns out the trees
are the main characters
of the earth story. People scurry around
like a VHS on fast forward and
will stick around about as long.
We'll be a metaphor
the trees use in stories they
tell each other over time while
watching the rats grow large.

III.

The tree
reached up, out,
every day.
Threw everything
into higher & *higher*,
into sun & *sun*.
Until, too big
for itself,
it fell.
Cracked & broken.
Prone & jagged.
It will feed the forest
if left alone
to its demise,
a textbook in its skin.

IV.

When we have to pause our hike
for a short-legs break, we look far in
beyond the trail edge
at trees, trees, trees.

I tell my boys about
leaves & sun, roots & water,
even xylem & phloem quickly
while I have some attention.

I tell them to never
tear off the bark.
"That's like if someone ripped off your skin,"
I say, accidentally terrifying
one and making the other
bust a gut. Little boys—
who can know?
Until puberty at least, when
every move is painfully predictable
for the coming decades.
But now, at seven and three,
wonder still permeates
and all is not lost.

Hungry, we head back.
The three-year-old says to them,
"Thank you, trees."
My boys spot
a short one up ahead—
they run & climb it,
shining in the sun.

When we get back,
they eat PB&J and apples
and laugh, laugh, laugh.
Hungry,
I laugh with them
while we still can.

Leaves

Yet another
unarmed Black man
was killed last week
by officers sworn to protect him

and a moment ago
my Black son saw me
looking concerned &
he shrieked "I'ma get you,

Daddy!" & tackled
me in the family room, his blankie
flying behind him like a flag.
We laughed until we calmed

and we cuddled and
carpet tickled our ears and
we looked out the window and
I showed him the buds

on the big, snow-dusted maple
that looms over our yard,
explained how soon
our tree will have leaves again.

"But where the old ones?" he asked,
"the ones that gone but
were there?" and
we talked about how they're

becoming mulch for the garden
by now, a long winter later,
how leaves were there before
but now aren't,

how new ones are coming soon,
how what is gone
will feed us over time,
how what is gone

isn't gone but is

Matters

The workshop asked
"At what age *is* it
appropriate to teach a
lesson on Emmett Till?"

The question sat, wary,
in the middle of the room,
pondered & surrounded.
The well-meaning began

to wrestle the question.
They aimed for an answer,
but an answer
is a form of defeat

and this is a question
to gather & hug tight.

This is a question
to hold, to rub its
head while
it's pulled out of the river,
to cradle while the
water pours out &
then drips until
it stops
altogether
when the question
finally
exhales.

We Hold These Truths

I dream of my children sleeping through nights,
warm in blankets they've burrowed underneath
with certain unalienable Rights.

Like any father worried about frights,
I fret for their safety to the umpteenth.
I dream of my children sleeping through nights.

We pile books by bedsides, preparing for slights,
ready to brandish words free of their sheaths
with certain unalienable Rights.

But will the future pull guns, ready for fights
when my Black sons grow large, hit their sixteenths?
I dream of my children sleeping through nights.

They grow in a time that has seen all sights
but plows ahead, the good buried beneath
with certain unalienable Rights.

I carry deep sighs & hope for great heights—
the daytime is long on every Juneteenth.
I dream of my children sleeping through nights,
with certain unalienable Rights.

Descent

How many corners are there in a brain? How much can hide in there? Earlier today someone mentioned those Absolut ads from every magazine in the '90s—how many of those ads lurk, forgotten? The corners of my brain must hold 500 Absolut ads like some bottle-shaped papier-mâché speakeasy door covering what I really want to remember with marketing bullshit, and right now, somewhere in my brain is the name of the non-André 3000 member of Outkast, and this I want to remember, but my synapses aren't playing. His name is hiding behind an Absolut Atlanta ad where a crowd of Braves fans sit in the shape of a bottle, doing the Tomahawk chop and hollering about how John Rocker played the game "the right way." My synapses are kids looking at their desks instead of the teacher's eyes. My synapses pretend they don't hear me when I shout "Are you even listening?" My synapses refuse to check the corners. My synapses are aiding and abetting my descent. I listened to the entirety of *Aquemini* last night while driving to and from a basketball game that we lost by four, and still, I got nothing, and surely he says his name somewhere in *Aquemini*, but his name has already walked slowly down the steps of my brain and hidden itself in a dark basement corner, behind that Absolut door and next to a box of comics full of characters I'll never remember either & a stack of VHS tapes from Michigan's championship run in '89, of which I'll remember next to nothing either. The rest of the basement is drowned out by 30,000 Braves fans robbing Mark Morrison & shouting

> Return of The Man
> Return of The Man
> Return of The Man

as they shift, like a tight marching band at halftime, from that Absolut bottle to that White Power hand sign they keep catching white boys doing in the White House because what, you thought they wouldn't appropriate gang signs too? So I refuse to look up these names because maybe just maybe my

synapses aren't dumb, maybe they're hiding beauty in the basement, away
from the Nazis, maybe in all the dark corners, my synapses bear hug
Ororo Munroe & Loy Vaught & Big Boi,
waiting, breathing, flexing, tense.

Last Laugh

The gas pump talked at me this morning. It
warned of war. It said bombs could fly at
any moment. Forget your books & classes,
says our society. Forget your learning,

says our culture. We'd rather repeat our
history over and again, hugging
the known no matter how horrible.
I maneuver our horseless carriage over

rivers and through the memories of woods
and past strip malls and the ghosts of woods and
by fast food and the phantom limbs of woods
to a Christmas party, toward the memories

my boys will hold when they take their own
nuclear crews to maybe my house if
I make it that far. If we make it that far.
I know more than most gas pumps. I'm older now,

I've gained wisdom. Like when people say *He
who laughs last, laughs best* but I know that's untrue—
nobody's really last because laughs pass,
contagious, like how now at the party

I have a warm drink that may or may not
have a smidgen of whiskey dolloped in
it, and I laugh like my father laughs and
my grandpa laughed—and that was the only

day of the year my grandpa laughed, but he
did, for that day—but now the gas pump asks.
Will my boys laugh like I do and their kids
like them? After the gas pumps tell the dusty

air of the fires? Will my future brood scavenge
from our endless dumps, will they huddle under
crumbled bridges and in hulking frames where
offices used to be, will they take time

for one day per year, at least, to be with
family however they define that
and laugh?

2

Homecoming

The prodigal son
returned yesterday

draped in the flag
shipped via Army freight

saluted by Taps and
a mother's wailing

as his procession
lumbered across the runway
unphotographed.

There will be no robe or ring.
There will be no feast of fatted calf.

Just some cold cuts and potato salad
back at the church

on Tuesday.

To Judge the Living and the Dead

When reading *Walden*,
the students rage—*rage*—against Thoreau,
like the man shot their
dogs one by one, moviemafioso-style.
They call him a fake,
a phony, a poseur,
try to outdo each other's bile
when they find out his cabin was only
a mile or two
from town;
call him an idiot
for the whole enterprise;
call him a nerd for
having no friends,
a *loser* for his experiment in
isolation.

But would the students say the same
if Thoreau,
in the manner they've
grown up with,
had divulged his personal business first,
if the book didn't start with
When I wrote the following pages,
or rather the bulk of them,
I lived alone, in the woods,
        but with
After my best
friend, my brother John,
died—RIP, JT—I needed to be

alone, to build
something, to tend some beans,

just to tend
some beans for a while, you know

      instead?

Muertos

Daddy will you come to
my party when I die?
   he said.
Um...what?
   I said.
My—what do you call
it—funeral?
Will you come to that?
   he said.
Bub, you're going to live
to be an old man & I'll be long gone by then,
   I said through my
   throat full of scarabs.
No, I want you to live
to be 80 million years old,
   he said.

   We paused & no one
   spoke while we let a
   song about loss slide
   out the radio and
   waited for my wife to
   come out of the bakery
   with a cake.
   We watched the rain
   stream down the car
   windows. Two miles away
   we were an hour late to a
   birthday party.
   From the womb of the car,

        we watched the suburbs
        chew up everything
        outside.

Will you come back for
the Day of the Dead at least?
            he said.
You bet,
            I said.
            Yo espero que sí.

Monumental

I stepped off the Metro
in March to a sea of teenagers
still holding their signs:
*"I'll miss my friends more
than you'll miss your guns."*

Their faces alive with voice,
their eyes beacons of belief,
the students straggled toward home, the protest over.
They walked past monuments to
war & to warriors.

> Thirty-five children & teachers
> have been torn to death
> by bullets at school this year.
> It is not yet summer.
> Seniors graduate today.

The children hollered
at the Capitol, brandished slogans—
"Protect us, not guns"—openly carried their
signs high above their heads,
packing words with pride.

> In 2013, the Advanced Placement English
> Language & Composition exam asked
> students to write an essay that would
> "examine the factors a group or agency should consider in
> memorializing an event or person and in creating a monument."

I walked down the mall as
students marched away past monuments to
war to war to war, holding their signs:
"The scariest thing in a school
should be my grades."

      476,277 students wrote an essay
      that year explaining what's worth
      memorializing, what merits a monument—
      this year thirty-five kids & teachers died, shot
      at school, more Americans

      dead at school than war but who's at war, really.
      We have enlisted grunts
      without their permissions or sixteenth birthdays.
      "Examine the factors a group or agency should consider in
      memorializing an event or person and in creating a monument."

      "I've never really thought about that
      before" the students said, but

they have now
as they laugh together,
ready to bury yesterday for tomorrow.

Ghost Ballad

an upright piano with no lid
sits by the side of the road
a hundred yards from the lake.

it is sun-bleached & warped
with no 90° angles—
the wood bending & curving like

the nearby trees. its sprung wires
grow long & reach out to twine
with the thin curious branches.

rainwater drips off what keys
are left as the piano groans in the strong
winds dragging behind the storm.

come by—
the song is yours
if you want it—

this piano sitting by the
side of the road, playing
dead music in the breeze.

Sam Cooke Said a Change Is Gonna Come

Sunfall
an autumn
maybe the words
    stopped
      for a reason
west wind
water spray
maybe it's time
    change
      is in season
moon rise
late night dew
maybe there's too
    much fear to
      listen. Words stop

revolutions
which solution

change is in season
pushing pushing
and crushing

just try to listen
try to breathe
changes seethe

for a reason.

3

Lake Huron, June 2017

A storm
the size of the horizon
was blowing in,
loud & dark as revelation.
We saw it engulf the islands
seven miles out.
I swam toward it,
stood on the sandbar,
and felt the sky turn so dark
it made the lake shine silver.

I watched the lightning hit the lake
while I was in the lake
and the storm was coming fast.

I would have stayed,
witness to the glory.
Her panicked voice cut
across the water &
asked me to come in, so

I looked to the lightning
again—then,
I submerged & swam
to the sand,
to my laughing boys
and my wife.

The wind turned
and blew the storm

east & away,

and the water sat
motionless & expectant.

New Day Rising

After Hüsker Dü

Deep shadows
cast by new sun
quiver
as the indiscriminate torch
rises
and burns off last night,
leaving only the ash of morning dew.

The LeBroniverse (Brought to You by Gatorade)
For Carrie

My wife & I sat at the
water's edge looking up at
the stars

      and what more can be said about
      the awe & immensity of the stars
      whose names were given at the dawn
      of Western civilization yet we still use
      today, which,

      all things considered
      is for the best because
      can you imagine what bullshit
      we'd come up with if we
      got to name the constellations
      today?

      "Oh look, you can see Mickey & Minnie
      really well tonight, right off to the
      east, next to The
      Beatles meteor shower."

      But oh come on, who am I kidding—
      It'd just be Budweiser Major & Verizon Minor &
      instead of the Milky Way it'd be
      the Milky Way™
      and so on for $1,000,000,000 each
      in naming rights.

But even if we managed to make the
stars ridiculous,
we still couldn't,
really.

They're too mind-boggling,
too magnificent,
too incomprehensible.

　　　Yet, in the face of immense awe,
there she & I sat
arguing about whether or not
to leave one of our son's cheap plastic toys
at my in-laws' cottage.
We could discuss infinity
or a $5.00 knock-off Lego train
and I'll be damned if we didn't
choose the train & what an
asshole I am

and she may be right & probably is,
but just look, look at
how beautifully her eyes reflect
　　　the shimmering of the Coca-Cola cluster in the northern sky.

Thank God for Ozzie Smith

When Dad chastised my brother & me for watching TV
on those gorgeous summer Saturdays,
I couldn't disagree, but
baseball beckoned
and any chance to watch our Tigers
    or *This Week in Baseball*
was too much to pass up.
It added up, those hours of
Willie Stargell homers, Pete Rose dives, Nolan Ryan no-hitters, and
Ozzie Smith back flips. It filled our mental record, and

it paid off.

When my two-year-old son ran
too hastily
to the top of the stairs and
tumbled head-first,
I laid out like Ozzie—
a dive so true I
paused
horizontal to the floor just long enough to realize
I was horizontal to the floor
with outstretched arms, and
I caught his right ankle
and held my grasp.

Ozzie, at that point, would pop to his feet
& zip a bullet to first or flip a popcorn
kernel into the mouth of the second baseman's glove
for a double play,

but I pulled in my catch,
held this bawling boy in the acreage of my palm,
rubbed his head,
and muttered love, love, love.

The inning over, I set him down to
toddle off with tentative steps,
and my heart & soul
did a standing back flip in celebration
of the golden magic of perfect movement,
a thank you
to grace.

So You'd Better Pay Attention

Seven years old and can't tie a shoe,
he grabs his mitt
and asks to shag flies.
The little league championship
is on the line tomorrow.

"Throw grounders now, Dad."
He gobbles them up, whips 'em back,
all gameface and dives a day early.

He struggles catching to his left, refuses
to just open up and stick his mitt
out to his left. He tries it
at last and of course it works—
his eyes go nova. "Again!"
And I throw it again & again.

I don't tell him I'm going to
and I heave one high.

Later I'll tell him that in baseball
you never know where the ball
will go so you have to be ready
for anything because you only know
that it will be pitched. You
have to wait, only knowing that
eventually the ball will take flight and
cruise like a missile
at a first-grader.
Eventually it all will take flight and

cruise like an asteroid
at you.

He squinted into the June sun.
He parsed cloud and maple leaf
and the pinpoint of baseball
falling,
period then iris then nickel then
baseball.

Then a cloud of dust
popped from his mitt
and drifted away.

There Is No News Cycle on the Trail
For Charlie

The world
went farther into the
handbasket's Hell today,
no doubt,
but forgive me
for not noticing this time.

You see,
it's late November in
Michigan, the time
when Joe Henry says you
can almost see the river
turn to steel,

and as a native son,
I vouch
he's right

because Charlie & I hiked
two hours today
and spent a good chunk
of time tossing sticks
through the
lake's grey skin.
All life was still except for
flying sticks, the ripples,
and a few curious deer who
watched us from afar, twitching white tails at
the imperceptible breeze.

The lake cares not

for problems.
Neither do the deer.
Neither, for that matter,
does my young son,
as impressed with each of my throws as he was with the first
because I can get the sticks

all the way to the water
past the ten feet of muck—
this true miracle replayed
a dozen times,
each splash
as incredible as the last—
"You did it!"

The lake teaches us this much at least—

you can
hurl dead wood
beyond the muck
to still water beyond.
And you can do it
again
& again
& again.

4

The Farm in Spring

I. Then

The May wind blows and
diesel fumes shimmer in the
sunrise. The fields wait.

Sunset brings us home.
Shower, then Steinbeck or Eisner
and bats overhead.

Fourteen hours in a
truck. A fox darts through June's tall
alfalfa, taunting.

Come August, back down
I-96 to college.
Highways take us away.

II. Now

Every May, I drive
to work in shirt & tie but
my bones look for the barn.

Every fall I hear
the goldenrod whispering
fool fool fool fool fool.

A Jackass Offers an Apology

I offer my sincerest apologies to my fellow motorists
because, see, I turned left in front of oncoming traffic—
in a snowstorm no less—
thinking I had a green left-turn arrow when, in fact,

I had only a standard green light and
a head full of worries—a wife & child with the flu,
a pay cut looming, a to-do list
too long to get done.

But there is no excuse for almost smashing up
a half-dozen cars in four inches of grimy
rush hour slush like my toddler would do
with his trucks in the basement carpet pile,

and I am sorry for being that driver,
the guy I would normally scream at
with the unholy fervor of the frustrated & angry
whose perceived wrongs erupt and

splash vitriol & spittle across
the inside of so many windshields.
I accept my deserved curses,
though I am sorrier yet for yelling at

others those hundreds of times before
because, oh, how we hope to simplify our world
by yelling, but, oh, how miserably,
how sadly, we fail and fail and fail

despite the continued flying of our birds,
those egocentric flags—
angry exclamation points jabbing out the windows
where scared, tentative question marks would be
more accurate,
more honest.

Heartbeats

Shoes laced, he picked up the ball,
started dribbling it
slowly at first, softly,
then firmer,
controlled & rhythmic.
He drove the ball down

and it snapped back to
his hand—
right, left, then crossovers,
between the legs,
behind the back,
sprints up & down the court.
Dribbling & paradiddling
a boombap.

Wood of old forests on
the floor, clay of old earth
in the bricks.
The gym itself a womb,
the dribbling ball,
its steady beat, and
amniotic sweat flew
off his brow
in the labor of
early summer heat.

A Jackass Tells a Story about Rivers

Tell a story about rivers, they said,
and of a thousand rivers—dreamed & real—
I am in one, amniotic & amnesiac,
dragging drunken feet through

three feet of water a half mile to the
lake where there is a bonfire,
a beach party on Lake Michigan
in Michigan where a certain brand

of person can only enjoy the lake
by tearing it apart with motors,
but these weren't those people. Oil
and tires didn't tell the stories of their day.

Deep night turned its blind eye to the beach & the bottles.
A guitar and a radio, and nobody caring about
competing notes that floated & banged
across & around each other before

reaching for the pines past the dunes and
the stars past the world. She started talking to me
and talked some more until she touched. This was one
of those times a lifetime ago when lives overlapped,

an intersection of rivers.
Say what you will about the brutalism of streets,
at least they tell you where to go—
signs command ONE WAY or STOP.

The warm waters just say *stay, stay*.
The currents make only suggestions.
I stumbled back, splashed through the river,
feet through dark muck, dissipating.

Balance

Yes, it was pure
poetry this morning
when I dropped
baseline, slipped my defender,
stretched my arm out in my
best white-boy Dr. J,
and laid in the basketball
reverse off the glass,
but it was also
poetry when I propelled
myself skyward like
a water buffalo trying
to break loose of
earthly bounds, missed the rebound,
came down on Raf's foot,
twisted my ankle, and fell
to the hardwood like a dropped stack of papers,
my soul a loose ball
bumping slowly off the bleachers.

A Jackass Learns to Call Them Groundhogs Now

At 14—with a plume of dust
a football field high & wide
behind me—I learned to drive. I
ground the gears of a decrepit grain
truck again & again, barreling the empty
red behemoth up & down the lanes
between fields.

> Corn to the east.
> Beans to the west.
> Curious birds darting.

The truck's wooden walls rattled
like bones put back to work.
Dad had given me instructions, had
demonstrated the how-to before he
hopped out to head back up to the farm.

> *Stay until you got it.*
> *Don't drive over crops.*
> *If you see a woodchuck, don't swerve.*
> *They dig holes by the creeks and*
> *cause breakdowns.*
> *And don't go by the creeks.*

Every summer after, when running hay
cuttings, the woodchucks played chicken
with my truck where the culvert goes under
the dirt road. The rocks pinged off the

metal tube the frogs hid their brood under.

       I never hit a single woodchuck,
       not for lack of trying.

Twenty years later, when I moved
to the suburbs, a woodchuck sat
by the side of Farmington Road
watching shiny F-150s with empty beds
roar by the cracked asphalt.
I watched him and the
river valley yawning behind him,
a deep green stripe between the streets.

       I gave him the farmer wave & nod,
       and when he moved, I swerved
       away.

At Sunset

with Dirk Schulze

When I do retire,
I don't look at it as a big celebration,
  riding off in the sunset smiling
  with dancing and music playing in the background.

To me, it's not that. Retirement
is depressing.

Depressing.

It's one of those things where
It's not something you want to do;

nobody wants to retire from basketball.
  You want to play basketball forever.

It's the end of something great, giving up something
I've been doing all my life, something
I've been striving for,
  trying to be the best at.

And now you got to say, 'I'm no longer that'?

I don't need a party. When I'm ready to go,

just let me go

A Jackass Reads Breaking News

There is a headline on a news
site today declaring
"Who inspired this celebrity's new
tattoo?" that might
as well have said
"Hoo boy, you're old"
because I have no idea
who the pictured celebrity is
or why I am supposed to care about the tattoo.

There are two hundred
or so other crises happening now,
entire peoples and nations at risk,
a nuclear reactor on the brink
& a glacier dribbling down the sink.

But the tattoo earns a headline
beside them all.

       It's a little heart,
       by the way.

Yes, this is attention paid to fame instead of future,

but I can't help but wonder
who merits this little inked heart
on someone's skin,

       who is loved
       today.

Three-Pointer

The lithe man with
giraffe necks for legs & arms
rises up into the air
and fast as a snare crack
straightens dozens of moving parts
into a line with his
wrist & hand clapped like

a gooseneck and he
launches the basketball
into the air
the arcing journey to home

the shot is a lifetime
a beginning middle & end
in one motion

born in the cradle
of the hand & fingertips
that second ticked and
that wrist flipped
and the ball was sent into the world
to strive & reach toward

the heavens only to
inevitably
be pulled back to
earth and land and the hoop
where the nylon net strings snap

with the sting
of the clock.

So many goods and bads
come with resolution at long last—
sooner than anyone watching
with held breath would think,

like it or not,
the end
arrives,

victory & loss
at the same time,

and the only one
who always wins
is the end.

A Jackass Looks at the Dutch & Faces a Truth

The art museum poses
problems, but one
little one every time I go:
Do I go into the modern
wing for the broad
energetic strokes that
shock & invigorate,
or do I swing by the
Dutch masters and
commiserate? Today
the Dutch won,
their sorrowful downward gazes,
the bright and the
dark twisting around each other
just as it always has,
as it always will.

Look at van Ruisdael's Jewish
Cemetery, at bright
hope surrounded by dark death:
politicians' bombs or sugared veins,
one truth remains.

        Something gon' kill us all
                Time the Revelator
        Something gon' kill us all
                Hear him riding
        Something gon' kill us all
                Come on hear him riding
        Something gon' kill us all

Time the Revelator
need be no book of the seven seals

Storm & sun
same for everyone

The Farm in Summer

I. Then

The grass dries & the
fireflies report on time.
The barn moos, scuffs hooves.

The stars hide behind
moonlight. Morning will bring wheat—
a field of sun—straw & bales.

We will sit again
at dusk, sweat soaked through it all,
bale-bloodied & breathing.

Come August, school calls.
People. Some new box. Return
to doors & ceilings.

II. Now

In June, I harvest
data. I file reports,
click SAVE on test scores.

Roll up my sleeves, run
a hand down inner forearms—
smooth smooth smooth smooth smooth.

5

[Attention Grabber Goes Here]

The teacher demanded the papers have five paragraphs,

tried to desperately cram rhizomatic life into five

measured compartments, tried to bake thought like cupcakes

with a formula desperate to make sense of it all, to

impose order while thought quietly sent itself sideways, underground.

We Should Do That

with Dirk Schulze

That'd be swell.
That'd be the cat's pajamas
The dog's ukulele
The fish's daydream about Erin Gray
The peach's new hi-def television set
The banana's favorite memorized poem
(which is probably "Bridge Over Troubled Water" because it lacks
imagination and never got past its sophomore-year lesson that focused only
on lyrics as poetry and never got to poetry as poetry the banana made
a very nice poster about the song, though, which still hangs on the upstairs
hallway wall, now yellowed around the edges)
The tree's 1952 Vincent Black Lightning
The soil's lasting memory of a white man razing its trees, planting wheat
& whatnot, then selling it off to whoever built this house with the frail
clay pipes under the yard leading to the sewer feed now all plugged
with new roots & dirt from revenge or time or does it matter which
The cow's hum & the horse's groan
The candle's dream of playing funk bass
The beer mug's longing for adventure
(like, maybe root a potato in me sometime or
something at least, eh, hoss?)
The tape measure's *Riverside Shakespeare*
The tomato's tchotchke
The worn sock's wistful memory of that warm afternoon in college
when winter finally turned to sun and slight breeze and sundresses and
light knees and laughing songs and a sprite's sneeze
and sundown, oh that slow slow sundown
The robin's drawings & the rabbit's still life
The cloud's go-to ballcap

The boulder's newspaper
The fascist's bathrobe
The American's dream
Or just the cat's pajamas.
It could be any one of them,
what do I know.

The Spine

While tromping the snowless woods
for a Christmas tree
I stepped on a deer's spine,
well, half a deer, really,
     which is another mystery in itself.
I called over my son, and
we perused every crag,
the zipper of the vertebrae,
the innumerable pores in the fractured skull.

When I die,
may I be left to rot,
to be found as bones
by the curious future and
     poked at with sticks,
even if for only a minute before
moving on to whatever task is at hand then.
May I be a healthy reminder
of awe
and intricacy.

Working

The brown water
asks you to go look at its blue cousin
somewhere instead
a great lake maybe
or the ocean
one of those prima donnas
but not this brown river
while it does its work

Why I Peed Outside with the Dog

Because a star
will never shine through
the bathroom ceiling.

There are other reasons—

brisk air & cold grass,
the corona of the moon,
I had to let out my brown dog
to do the same anyway—

but all the evidence really
needed is now penetrating
the cloudless atmosphere:

the pre-Precambrian
light, emitted by stars
that died before Time & now falling
through the naked branches
of the maple tree.

Who am I to seclude
myself from bearing
witness?

Fungus

For Franklin

I

Bigs & I
ditch the car
and dive into the trail
that runs parallel to that highway
a hundred yards beyond the trees.
(Oh, Suburbs, sometimes you forget
a spot and the sprawl
goes around it,
and I thank you for
your inattention to detail.)

Torrential rains last week,
deep mud today.
My four-year-old, unable to stay
upright in the slick,
so I piggyback him for
most of the hour we're back here.
Water streaked with oil & rainbows
trickles over my boots.

We pause to examine a spot of land.
He is fascinated by dead trees,
convinced that only lightning
& tornadoes could knock over
such towering majesties.
I don't explain to him yet
how maples grow easy as weeds here

and blow over like a dollar-store
birthday candle.
He says, "The dirt is dead people!"
and we talk about how soil
is dead everything—
sure, a small amount of it
people, I guess, but more so
dead plants, a few animals, lots of insects,
and the glaciers' boulders
now ground to dust.

I tell him how dead trees bring even more life
to the woods than living trees,
and we examine fallen trunks:
insects, a fungus, decomposing bark & wood.
He pokes at the fungus &
says "fungus."
When he looks up,
he sees a tree chewed away by deer,
the heartwood exposed & orange,
bright.

II

We spy a deer off the trail—
long after the nonplussed doe
had spotted us—and
she watches, waiting.
Bigs, nonplussed right back,
shouts "FUNGUS" & the deer
returns to munching spring's new shoots.

He now knows about fungus, so
he shouts from my back at
every downed tree

YOU HAVE FUNGUS. After dozens
of dead trees & their fungus,
he tires & rests his head
on my shoulder.

Large & strong for his age,
his trunk goes limp as he nods
off, his flesh soft.
He says, "I love trees," and I say I do too,
and he says, "I love you," and I say I love
him too and the pause

doesn't last long because
now he is upright again,
pivoting to see into the trees
as he determines what exactly out here
a deer would eat.
She'd eat that but not that, he says
with no antecedents.

III

We say *bye* to the river
and he says, "The river can't talk!"
We pause & listen to the river
speaking in original tongues.
It is hard to hear with the
highway screaming in the background.
There are car parts in the river.
A plastic chunk of a car gathers
bottle caps like a nanny
hugging children.

He has reconsidered.
"The river has a face, and the

river sounds like this" he says, grumbling
in a deep voice. Then, quiet for a bit,
and he says, "I'm sorry.
It doesn't," and he is embarrassed
by his figurative language.
I pounce & push away the hungry
dog of our culture trying to swallow
my four-year-old.
I say,

"The river can have a face & a voice,
Big Man, and don't you let
anyone tell you it can't. There are more languages
than ours and more words than humans can hold."

He happily speaks in river for the next
500 yards until
he returns to FUNGUS
and he shouts FUNGUS
at more dead trees he shouts
FUNGUS at the air he shouts
FUNGUS at the sky & clouds he
shouts FUNGUS at each & every
one of the invisible stars
beyond

until we are back to cars
and we go home.

6

A Tree, Again

In 1989 when I was still in high school, I read an article about carbon &
warming, so this

is nothing new.
For long enough
that it's tradition,
people have waved
banners & worn
t-shirts that shout
Save the Planet,
but the planet will
remain and suffice for
the cockroaches & mice.

My older son fell asleep asking questions about god & heaven. My younger
son screamed

awake at 3:30 a.m.
I told them both,
"Go to sleep now,
baby. We'll talk
tomorrow" and
rubbed their backs
till they relaxed.
We'll talk
tomorrow, but
will we.

When I read that back in '89, I went out on the lawn next to a massive,
dying maple tree and

stared at the night sky
with my red dog beside me.
Stars we could still see.
I wondered then
what was wrong
with the older generations
that they could ignore this
but still
now
good lord

still now
good lord
how
good lord
still
good lord
still
good lord
still
good lord
still
good lord
still
good lord
still
good lord
still
good lord
still
good lord
still
good lord
still
good lord
still
good lord

still
good lord
still
good lord
still
good lord
still
good lord
still
good lord
still
good lord
still
good lord
still
good lord
still
good lord
still
good lord
still
good lord
still
good lord
still
good lord
still
good lord
still
good lord
still
      be still
       be still
        be slit
          throats singing
           spilling and
             done with it.

Ashen

They had a point.
It's easier to pretend.
Nicer. Have you tried
explaining to your kid
what's happening? More
so, what's about to happen?
What *is* about to happen?

I'll explain it to you again,
bud. We'll do our best
while it burns. We'll compare
the flame to the sunsets we
watched over the bay. We'll
talk about how the embers
of what we'll then realize
had been the world

float off after dark like
orange fireflies, like lightning
bugs when we had seas
of them, like tiny sunsets
blinking out, finally cooling in the
dark, when no one was there
to watch.

Winter

was quiet like the mouse tunneling next to our foundation.
Everyone's happy except the lost. It started
getting light too soon. Spirits tried to wander in
the bare branch shadows, the moon & trees printed on
the ground, negatives. But spring's breath was already
the wind. Some of the spirits rode off on the jetstream
when it went away. Gone. Now some of us left
stay up a little late, confused. Raise a toast.
Watch the cold dark
lose itself.

Untitled

I.

How we bask in that
spring ray of sun,
windows down, radio up.
How we try to breathe,
try to relax a shoulder,
rub a temple, while
we burn fuel and
our fraying souls,
smoldering at the edges,
about to catch.

II.

We were in Arizona a couple times (after they moved there) when we were kids. We went to some guy's house. He might've been (a distant relative or) a member of their church. These things were never clear. His freezer was full
      of dead rattlesnakes, coiled & cold. Dominion, shot & sealed.

III.

And we all race around the surface streets hoping to catch the one green light that will get us somewhere fast enough to fix everything. Held breath hoping there's still time if we burn it.

IV.

Before bed, Bigs played
"Three Little Birds" on
a ukulele the school
sent home. All passion
& little accuracy and no one cared.
"He died young," he said and
"That's true," I said.
"That's sad," he said and
"I agree," I said.

In the cool morning above
the parking lot at work,
three crows sit atop a
light pole, barking at the
students & teachers, their caws
dissipating little clouds
over our heads.

V.

And now I'm just a bag of memories.

Notes

A general note that may impact several poems in this book: My wife and I are white adoptive parents to Black sons. Some of these poems address parenting anxiety around raising Black boys in racist America.

In "The Trees," the quote "what is it when / a death is ruled a homicide but / no one is responsible for it" comes from a tweet by Hanif Abdurraqib.

The poem "Descent" cites John Rocker. Rocker was a pitcher for the Atlanta Braves baseball team who served a 14-game suspension in 2000 for racist and homophobic comments in an interview in *Sports Illustrated* magazine.

"Monumental" was first drafted in 2018. According to reports, that year 14 U.S. soldiers died by hostile action, and 43 children and adults died in U.S. school shootings.

The poem "Sam Cooke Said a Change Is Gonna Come" can be read in both lines and columns. Sam Cooke's song "A Change Is Gonna Come" became an anthem in the Civil Rights Movement upon its release in 1964.

This Week in Baseball, cited in "Thank God for Ozzie Smith," was a weekly baseball highlights show. It was popular in the 1980s when sports news wasn't available 24/7, and it introduced kids like me to all-stars we might not have seen otherwise, such as the players in the poem.

"There's No News Cycle on the Trail" cites Joe Henry, an American singer-songwriter and Grammy-winning producer who spent some of his formative years in Michigan. His song "Sault Saint Marie" includes the line "You can almost see the river in November turn to steel."

"At Sunset" is a found poem from "Still at work," Jo-Ann Barnas's article about Detroit Piston Ben Wallace, Detroit Free Press, April 22, 2012.

The painting cited in "A Jackass Looks at the Dutch & Faces a Truth" is Jacob Isaaksz van Ruisdael's *The Jewish Cemetery*. It is in the collection at the Detroit Institute of Arts and can be seen online at https://dia.org/collection/jewish-cemetery-60034. It is an imposing almost six feet tall by seven feet wide including its ornate frame. Also in this poem, the "Time the Revelator" lines owe a debt to Son House's version of the blues standard "John the Revelator" and Gillian Welch's *Time* (*The Revelator*).

If my children ever read "Why I Peed Outside with the Dog," boys, you should absolutely use the toilet and only the toilet, and put the seat up first.

"A Tree, Again" cites a cover article about global warming (as we called it then) from *Newsweek* magazine. We have no excuses. We have known for my entire adult life and then some.

Acknowledgements

Thank you to the editors of the following publications in which these poems appeared, some in earlier versions or under different titles. A number of these poems were first drafted in the Tupelo Press 30/30 Project.

Barstow & Grand: "The LeBroniverse (Brought to You by Gatorade)"

Blue Mountain Review: "Heartbeats"

Dunes Review: "Farm in Spring" and "Sam Cooke Said a Change is Gonna Come"

8 Poems: "Lake Huron, June 2017"

English Journal: "Homecoming" and "[Attention Grabber Goes Here]"

Exposition Review: "Descent" A special thank you to the editors for nominating "Descent" for Best of the Net 2019.

433 Mag: "We Hold These Truths"

HAD: "We Should Do That," "So You'd Better Pay Attention," and "The Spine"

Language Arts Journal of Michigan: "Thank God for Ozzie Smith" and "To Judge the Living and the Dead"—*Cobalt Review* re-published "Thank God for Ozzie Smith" in their 2018 baseball issue

The Night Heron Barks: "He Looks at the Dutch & Faces a Truth" and "Leaves"—*Blue Mountain Review* re-published "Leaves"

Nurture: "Fungus"

Olney Magazine: "A Jackass Offers an Apology"

Outrider Press: "Why I Peed Outside with the Dog"

Paddler Press: "A Jackass Learns to Call Them Groundhogs Now"

Rise Up Review: "Matters"

Roanoke Review: "Muertos"

Rockvale Review: "There is No News Cycle on the Trail"

STAND Magazine: "At Sunset"

Sunspot Literary Journal: "The Trees, Part I"

UCity Review: "A Jackass Reads Breaking News," "A Jackass Tells a Story about Rivers," "Ghost Ballad," and "Last Laugh"

West Texas Literary Review: "Air Show"

Wine Cellar Press: "Monumental"

Words & Sports Quarterly: "Balance" and "Three-Pointer"

I'll start by admitting there are more people deserving of thanks than I'll be able to remember. Thank you all, sincerely, beginning with you, the reader. The whole reason a writer even seeks publication is to complete the circuit with you.

Thank you to my parents, Ken and Liz Nobis, for their lifelong support. Thank you also to my brother, Kerry. None of this would've happened if we didn't grow up surrounded by books, magazines, comics, newspapers, cereal boxes, catalogs, and everything else with words that we devoured.

An immense thank you to RD Morgan and Snežana Žabić at Match Factory Editions for everything. Your grace and editorial insights are invaluable. Match Factory feels like a home.

Big thanks to two early readers, Jared Beloff and Shannon McLeod, who graciously read and provided feedback on a much earlier version of this book.

Thank you to the entire online poetry community. I don't want to leave anyone out, so I'll just say if we've posted, texted, emailed, or DMed to talk shop together, I'm indebted to you, and thank you. In particular, thank you to the NAWP community, including my co-founder Jared Beloff again.

I could thank many friends, but I need to name one specifically. Thank you, Dirk Schulze—our correspondences over the years are probably the best writing I'll ever do.

An immeasurable thank you to Janet Swenson. This book wouldn't exist without your encouragement years ago. Thank you also to everyone else in Red Cedar Writing Project for years of writing and revising with me.

To Carrie and to Charlie and Franklin: Thank you for my marvel of a life. Everything for you.

About the Author

Mitchell Nobis is a writer and K-12 public school teacher in Metro Detroit where he lives with his family and dog. He facilitates the Teachers as Poets group for the National Writing Project, hosts the Wednesday Night Sessions reading series for KickstART Farmington, and co-founded the Not at AWP (NAWP) reading series. He is a past president of the Michigan Council of Teachers of English and former co-director of Red Cedar Writing Project, and he co-authored *Real Writing: Modernizing the Old School Essay*, a pedagogical text for writing teachers. For more, see mitchnobis.com or find him falling apart on a basketball court.

www.ingramcontent.com/pod-product-compliance
Lightning Source LLC
Chambersburg PA
CBHW051325120626
46547CB00015B/2396